John Sinclair

Considerations on Militias and Standing Armies

With some observations on the plan of defence suggested by the Earl of

Shelburne, and some thoughts on the propriety of military exercises on

Sunday, and on the necessity of a Scotch militia

John Sinclair

Considerations on Militias and Standing Armies
With some observations on the plan of defence suggested by the Earl of Shelburne,
and some thoughts on the propriety of military exercises on Sunday, and on the
necessity of a Scotch militia

ISBN/EAN: 9783337409265

Printed in Europe, USA, Canada, Australia, Japan

Cover: Foto ©ninafisch / pixelio.de

More available books at **www.hansebooks.com**

CONSIDERATIONS

ON

MILITIAS

AND

STANDING ARMIES.

WITH

Some OBSERVATIONS on the PLAN of DEFENCE
fuggefted by the EARL of SHELBURNE, and fome
Thoughts on the Propriety of Military Exercifes on
Sunday, and on the Neceffity of a SCOTCH MILITIA.

BY A MEMBER OF PARLIAMENT.

Where Men are unfit for War, the Fault is not in the Nature
or Situation of the Place, but in the Careleffnefs or Defect
of the Magiftrate. MACHIAVEL's Difcourfes, B. 1. Ch. 21.

ADVERTISEMENT.

WHEN the public at large feem to be peculiarly impreffed with the apprehenfion of depredations upon our coafts, it is furely unneceffary to make any apology for a publication of this nature. Notwithftanding the late glorious events in the Weft-Indies, we are ftill in point of naval force inferior to our enemies. It is neceffary, therefore, that we fhould improve our prefent imperfect fyftem of internal defence, otherwife we can neither be fafe at home, nor can we take effectual advantage, of the late happy turn, in the tide of our affairs.

The author has to regret that it is his misfortune to differ with a very refpectable ftatefman in regard to the propriety of arming the towns, becaufe he apprehends that fuch a fyftem may probably be the parent of popular diforders. As defence however, is the great object of every political fociety, notwithftanding the poffible danger of fuch a plan, it ought to be adopted, unlefs a better one can be eftablifhed in its room. He has ventured to ftate his opinion upon this fubject, and he hopes it will appear that exercifing

CONSIDERATIONS

ON

Militias and Standing Armies.

CHAP. I.

Of the different Modes of providing for national Defence.

ALL well governed ſtates ought ever to be prepared to defend themſelves, or to annoy their enemies. This cannot be effected without a military force. That force muſt either be perpetually in arms, or only diſciplined occaſionally. The firſt is termed a ſtanding army, the other a militia.

A ſtanding force is certainly attended with this advantage, that it does in general preſerve a great ſuperiority in the field, over *raw and undiſciplined militias.* But this circumſtance in its favour is counterbalanced by the many diſadvantages attending a ſpecies of defence, which is ſo expenſive to the ſtate, ſo deſtructive to induſtry, and dangerous to freedom.

B   The

The fatal experience of many ages, has fully proved the enormous expence of standing armies: Europe now groans under the many heavy burdens which they have occafioned; and inftead of decreafing, they are likely to become ftill more ruinous and oppreffive. Every prince (as Montefquieu well obferves) keeps as many armies in pay, as if he dreaded the extirpation of his people by a foreign invafion; and in proportion as one ftate augments the number of its troops, the neighbouring ftates of courfe do the fame; fo that none are gainers, and the ruin is general. The wealth and commerce of the univerfe not being able to counteract the baneful confequences of a fyftem which muft depend for its fupport upon the increafing taxes, and the oppreffion of the people.[*]

As ftanding armies are the props of arbitrary power, it is fcarcely poffible that they fhould not ultimately prove highly unfavourable to induftry; for though a nation, at the firft eftablifhment of military force, trufting to it for fecurity and protection, may for fome time apply itfelf to labourious employments, yet induftry can never be permanent where property is expofed to the plunder of a tyrant, or to military licentioufnefs.[†] Befides,

[*] Spirit of Laws, l. 13. c. 17.
[†] In arbitrary governments, no man is fecure in the enjoyment of what he has, and confequently no man is induftrious in acquiring property, or frugal to preferve it. And where military government is eftablifhed, it is by plunder
der

when a standing army is kept up, its labour is lost to the state during the whole year, even in time of peace, when it is a uselefs burden upon the nation; whereas a militia, according to our regulation, is exercised only one month in the year, and therefore in time of peace as much labour is lost to the community by keeping up fifty thousand regulars, as by six hundred thousand militia. But a militia, when properly regulated, is far from being so pernicious to industry.[*] For it either excludes artists and manufacturers, and is confined to husbandmen, who can spare a month's labour in the year without any public detriment; or it is exercised on festival days only, as is the case in Switzerland, when the men would otherwise be idle.

The taxes levied in order to support numerous bodies of mercenary forces, is one of the greatest checks that industry can meet with; for no man can toil with diligence, or with satisfaction, when he knows that a large proportion of his labour must go to the maintenance of men, who hold every species of industry in the highest ridicule and contempt. The natural confequence of this is, that

der that men expect to enrich themselves, not by industry or labour. Parliamentary Debates.

[*] Geneva and Switzerland may be cited to prove, that a well regulated militia is far from being incompatible with industry. Nay, the militia of Holland defeated the regular forces of Spain, and at the same time established those arts and that commerce which have since raised the United Provinces to their present flourishing situation.

the

the people take a diſlike to their occupations, and the wretched example of ſloth and inactivity ſhewn by the army, is ſoon followed by the reſt of the nation. Thus a ſtanding army is expenſive to a ſtate, whilſt at the ſame time it checks that induſtry, and dries up thoſe very ſources by which that expence can be ſupported.

But in a country like Britain, which boaſts of its liberty, and where I believe we are as free as we are entitled to be by our luxury and corruption ; this ſeems to be the ſtrongeſt objection to a ſtanding army, that the rights and privileges of a free people (if ſuch forces are eſtabliſhed) muſt indeed be precarious. *

In England it has been ſaid, as our army is commanded by men of family and fortune, who have an intereſt in the peace and civil proſperity of this nation, ſuperior to their private intereſt as ſoldiers, it is impoſſible that our liberties can be

* The individuals of which ſtanding armies are compoſed, are miſerable from the tyranny exerciſed over them, and are themſelves the cauſe of miſery to their fellow citizens from the tyranny they exerciſe. But it will be ſaid that they defend the nation from foreign enemies. Alas! could a foreign conqueror occaſion more wretchednefs than ſuch defenders. When he who calls himſelf my protector, has ſtripped me of my property, and deprived me of my freedom, I cannot retain him very cordial thanks, when he tells me, that he will defend me from every other robber. Moore's Travels, vol. 1. p. 195.

in

in any danger from them or thofe whom they command. But this is flippery ground to ftand on. For, in the firft place, our officers, like thofe of other armies are paid; nay, appointed by the crown and from that fource alone can expect to rife in their profeffion; they are fubjected to the orders of every fuperior officer almoft without limitation †, and if they refufe to obey, may be punifhed with death: nay, if in confequence of arbitrary fteps and oppreffive meafures being taken, any patriotic officer fhould attempt to throw up his commiffion, without leave from the crown, by the prefent laws, he might be tried by a court-martial and fhot as a deferter. ‡

Befides whatever the officers may be, every one muft acknowledge that the private foldiers of a ftanding army, are recruited from the very dregs of the people; who by idlenefs, extravagance and other vices, have been driven into the army. Such men might be apt to obey the commands of a

† By the Mutiny-Bill, officers are only bound to be obedient *to lawful commands*; but this is fo vague and in-definite an expreffion that fome explanation feems to be neceffary for the fecurity of men of public fpirit.

‡ In time of war, it might be dangerous to permit officers to throw up their commiffions, without leave from the crown; but in peace, when our liberties are moft likely to be attached, it might be permitted without any danger to the ftate.

fovereign

fovereign however unjuft and arbitrary, however oppofite to the intereft of the nation or the wifhes of their commanders. Even their fervice inftead of being confined to a certain number of years is unlimited and may laft for life *. Thus by denying them any profpect of regaining their fituations as citizens, we give them but little reafon to protect that freedom of which they do not partake. A ftanding army, therefore notwithftanding all our imaginary fafeguards, may be as dangerous to the liberties of Britain, as it has proved elfewhere, and unlefs a military fpirit is propagated among the people in general, if we efcape being conquered by a foreign enemy, we may expect to be enflaved by domeftic janizaries and a tyrannical fultan.

Nor are thefe the only difadvantages of a ftanding army; for if arms become a feparate profeffion, thofe who fubfift by them have an intereft directly oppofite to the intereft of the nation †. Wars and tumults, in many refpects advantageous

---

* Many unfuccefsful attempts have been made to fhorten the duration of a foldier's fervitude, and indeed there is a ftrange abfurdity in the idea of their being bound for life, if the army is only an annual one. Properly they can only be inlifted for one year, but that period may afterwards be prolonged by parliament.

† If foldiers are unjuftly accufed of exciting wars, they have not without reafon been condemned for protracting them when begun. Marfhall Byron's fentiment is too general in the army. " When the enemies of our kings are " conquered, their generals are no longer thought of. It
is

to the foldiers, are fubverfive of national felicity. In peace he is ufelefs and unemployed, whereas in time of war, he has in profpect laurels, plunder and preferment. Hence fays Machiavel, it is natural for a foldier to obftruct peace, and to urge on war, and therefore princes who wifh to prevent any diforders in the ftate, and are defirous of living in peace and fafety, ought to have their armies compofed of fuch perfons only, as will take up arms freely in defence of their country whenever neceffity fhould require, and when peace is concluded will as readily return to their former trades and occupations *.

But above all it ought to be remembered that if a ftanding army is long kept up in any country, it alters the very nature of the people. Tho' in former times they have ever been fo much renowned for courage and refolution, yet if they are for any time unacquainted with arms or unaccuftomed to difcipline, they become meer poltroons, terrified at the fight of a hoftile weapon, or the very name of a foldier; and to add to this evil, as the army muft be recruited from this daftardly and effeminate race, however formidable it may be to

" is our intereft therefore (fays he to his fon) to protract the
" war, that we may not be laid afide as unferviceable." Vide Bayle's Dictionary. Voce Gontaut (Armand de) Baron of Biron. Note. D.
* Vide Machiavel on the Art of War. l. 1. c. 4. Alfo Blackfton's Commentaries. Book 1. c. 13.

the unhappy people by whom it is fupported, it will never be able to defend their country againft a daring invader *. Such an army may be neceffary to ftates in poffeffion of diftant territories, or fond of foreign acquifitions; but a nation only inclined to defend itfelf, if its militia is well regulated fcarcely requires any other mode of protection. Such a difference there is between attacking an enemy's country, and defending our own.

In fact, an army acting on the defenfive only, and in full poffeffion of the country which is the theatre of war, has every advantage over its enemy. It can never be obliged to fight without the greateft probability of fuccefs; and whenever militias fail in defending their country, there will be more reafon to impute blame to the unfkilfulnefs of their generals than to the cowardice of the men. The greateft military exploits recorded in hiftory; namely, thofe of Marathon, Thermopylæ, Platæa, Morgarten, Sampach, Wefen, Creffy †,

* Any one who has read with attention the juftly celebrated hiftory of the decline and fall of the Roman empire, will feel the full force of this obfervation.

† The whole of Edward the Third's army, at the battle of Creffy, were new levied troops. Hume's Hift. vol. ii. 6—15. ann. 1346. And with fimilar forces, Henry the Eighth, at the famous battle of Guinegate or Spurs, defeated the army of France, tho' the officers were excellent and the foldiers had been long trained in the Italian wars. Vide Rapin's Hift. Vol. 1. b. 15. Machiavel's difcourfes. L. 1. c. 21.

I

Poictiers, and Agincourt, were performed not by ftanding armies, but by well trained militias, and the boafted Pruffian army itfelf principally con-fifts of a well difciplined militia, embodied for two or three months every year, and then difperfed to their ufual labours and occupations *.

.The great requifites of a foldier, are courage, difcipline and ready obedience, and thefe qua-lifications may be found in a well regulated mili-tia, nearly in as great perfection as in a ftanding army. As to perfonal courage, it is either found-ed on natural conftitution, on the hopes of honour and reward, and the fear of difgrace and punifh-ment, or fometimes on a contempt of danger found-ed on the remembrance of paft dangers which have been efcaped with fafety. It is this laft fpecies of courage only, which belongs peculiarly to a vete-ran army; for the reft may be found in a militia. But no kind of valour has been attended with fuch aftonifhing effects, as that enthufiafm of the mind which naturally arifes from a near connexion with the event. If perfonal intereft is at ftake, a man neither liftens to his fear, nor to his reafon. When he fights in defence of every thing that is dear and valuable, if his arms are fuited to the purpofe, and his efforts are well conducted he muft be fuccefsful†.

* Vide Moore's Travels. Vol. 2. p. 209.
† In general fome inftances of barbarity, either real or fictitious, or perhaps exaggerated, excite the rage and fpirit
C   of

By difcipline, I mean a thorough knowledge of the ufe of the inftruments of war, and the exercifes of a foldier. For, like other trades, the military one has its craft, pretending that difcipline cannot be acquired without long practice and experience, though innumerable inftances prove that the moft important parts of military exercife may be very fpeedily learned under proper direction. The articles of difcipline moft eflential for a foldier, according to Machiavel, are, to be inured to labour and hardfhips, which renders a man active and hardy ; to be taught how to handle and make ufe of arms ; and how to keep his ftation in the battalion he belongs to, without diforder or con-fufion.*

As to the firft article, it is certain that the foldiers of a well regulated militia are more accuftomed to labour, than any individual in the army ; for the former is in the conftant habit of maintaining himfelf by his own toil, whereas the regular foldier lives in idlenefs, fupported by the induftry of others. In this refpect, therefore, a militia feems to have a great advantage over a ftanding army.

With regard to the manual exercife of the fire-lock, a fufficient knowledge of it is far from being

of the invaded to fuch a pitch, that nothing but the want of proper arms and fkilful generals hinder their deftroying the enemy.

* Machiavel's Art of War, l. 2. c. 6.

difficult

difficult to acquire. A recruit, without being in the leaft acquainted with arms, may, to ufe a technical phrafe, be thoroughly drilled in a month's time. By experience he may ufe his weapons with more feeming dexterity, but not in a manner more deftructive. That fleight of hand, which is all his additional acquifition, is of no real fervice to him in action; for in battle, there is no time for juggling *.

As to the third article of military difcipline, a militia muft be inferior in that particular to a ftanding army; yet before an ifland, like Great-Britain, could be invaded by a powerful armament, there would be time fufficient to acquire it: and though it might be difficult to make a militia alert in all the little punctilios of a review, yet they may foon be made as fit for real action as any regular troops whatever, which have never before been in the field.

In a ready and implicit obedience to orders alfo, a militia is in general reckoned inferior to a ftanding army; but to this it may be anfwered, that a well regulated militia has its officers com-

* Well difciplined battalions are taught to fire at once, fo as to make but one report. This may do at a review to pleafe the populace, who judge of foldiers as they do of muficians, *by the ear*; but it is of no ufe in an engagement. Nay, it prevents the foldiers from taking an aim, or levelling their pieces according to the nature of the ground which they, and the enemy ftand on.

pofed

pofed of thofe who have influence and authority over their foldiers in time of peace, as well as in the field. Whenever that is the cafe, they are not inferior to ftanding armies, even in the article of obedience; and it is in general more perfect as it arifes from refpect and affection more than from fear of punifhment. Befides, if it were allowed that militias, particularly when ill-regulated, are inferior to ftanding armies in the article of obedience, yet it may be obferved in their favour, that by practice and experience that difadvantage is overcome, and that a few months of uninterrupted exercife in the field, will render them in every refpect equal to regular forces. This proves, that under an able general, and by fkilful management, they are fully equal to the defence of a nation. If the country be extenfive, its conqueft can never be effected in a fhort fpace of time, nor until the greateft part of the people may have become expert foldiers.

But whatever militias might be made by proper regulations, there is no reafon to wonder that in general they are reckoned infufficient for national defence, when we confider how little they are in general attended to, and how ill they are regulated. Their arms, their ammunition and other warlike neceffaries are moft commonly inferior to thofe of ftanding armies. The article of arms is of the firft importance to a foldier; for if by their means he is able to deftroy great numbers of the enemy,

all

all their skill and courage will not stand them in any stead *.

Nor would militias betray the trust reposed in them, if they were more depended on. But when standing armies are told, that every thing depends upon their valour, whilst the exertions of a militia are held forth to public ridicule and contempt, what can be expected from the latter ? Indeed as perpetual forces are favourable to the power of kings, and consequently adverse to the liberties of the subject, it is not improbable that militias are purposely neglected and ridiculed in order to render mercenary troops more necessary and less odious. In the words of a celebrated historian, it has long been the chief object of royal policy to increase and support standing armies. And the great aim of princes and ministers to discredit or annihilate every other means of national activity or defence †.

There are five methods by which European nations have hitherto protected themselves from invasion and conquest ‡; standing armies, foreign

---

* The success of the Romans with more justice may be imputed to their superiority in the nature of their arms, than in valour or discipline. In courage and discipline the Greeks and Macedonians were fully equal to the Romans, but the arms of the latter both offensive and defensive, were in many respects preferable, and hence their superiority proceeded.

† Robertson's Hist. of Charles the Vth. Vol. I. p. 95.

‡ In Asia, nations endeavour to provide for their security by establishing feudatory princes in the distant pro-

auxiliaries, fortifications, a navy, and a militia; and of thefe the laft on many accounts is entitled to a preference for the purpofe of internal defence.

As to ftanding armies, it has been already ob-ferved, that they are but a very uncertain fecurity againft foreign invafions. When regular forces alone are depended upon, whatever they may be as to courage and refolution, the reft of the nation muft be unwarlike. If by any accident therefore the ftanding army is defeated, there is no refource, but in fubmiffion: for diforderly multitudes unfkil-ful in the art of war, can never defend their pof-feffions againft the efforts of a bold and enterprizing enemy. Whereas, when every man is trained to be a foldier, the fate of an empire can never depend upon the iffue of a fingle engagement. This, Hannibal fatally experienced, when he at-tempted the conqueft of Italy; army after army he defeated, but new ones fucceeded. As long as every Roman was trained to arms, Rome remained in-vincible.

Foreign auxiliaries we know by experience in this ifland, is a mode of defence ftill more dan-gerous, and more expenfive, and at the fame time lefs to be depended upon. According to Sidney, they want either fidelity, or courage, and fometimes both. If they are not corrupted or beat by the

vinces, or by defolating their frontiers. But European empires are too confined for fuch modes of defence.

in-

invader, they make a prey of their mafters. Gain
and not right is their object, and their maxim,

" Ibi fas, ubi maxima merces"*

The very nature of an ifland prevents the neceffity of paying much attention to fortifications:
we feem however in this refpect to have paid too
implicit an obedience to the advice of Buchannan;
for if the towns upon the fea coaft were fortified,
it would undoubtedly tend to intimidate our enemies from attempting an invafion †.

Fleets are moving forts, and tho' I wifh not to
undervalue that bulwark of the trade and commerce of Great Britain, yet it muft be obferved
that they are far from being that fure fource of
internal protection which has been fo frequently
inculcated.

For in the firft place, fleets, at leaft ufeful ones,
muft entirely depend upon commerce. Without
trade, all the efforts of defpotifm cannot rear up a
formidable navy. But how uncertain and varia-
ble a thing commerce is, ancient as well as modern
hiftory informs us, and naval ftrength muft be
equally precarious.

---

* Sidney's political difcourfes, c. 2. fect. 23. Vide alfo
Harrington, p. 99. 184. 277. and 453.

† Buchannan's advice was, " Nec foffa, & muris pa-
triam, fed marte tueri." Though it were to be wifhed
fince we decline trufting to walls and ditches, that our
arms were under better regulation.

Secondly

Secondly, the materials of which ships are com‑
poſed are of a ſhort lived and periſhable nature,
requiring continual repair and uninterrupted at‑
tention. If therefore there are any pauſes of at‑
tention, or even a temporary neglect, your boaſted
fleet will very ſoon be annihilated, and dwindle
away of itſelf.

Thirdly, there is no kind of defence which in
general is ſo perfectly deſtroyed by an enemy, or
which it is ſo difficult to recover. One fortified
town may be taken, and yet the others are not
weakened. An army may be cut off, but in time
men may be diſciplined to ſupply their place.
But ſo difficult is it to repair the loſs both of ſhips
and of ſeamen, that if a fleet is ruined, either by
a ſuperior force, or by accident, years will not re‑
place it.

Fourthly, fleets are more liable to deſtruction
from the elements than any other ſpecies of defence.
To the baneful effects of earth, air, fire, and water,
they are almoſt equally expoſed. A defence de‑
pending upon any element is far from being a
certain one; but when it is ſubjected to more than
one, nay, to all the elements, it muſt indeed be
precarious.

Laſtly, even a ſuperiority at ſea, joined to all
the vigilance imaginable, will not always prevent
an invaſion; of this, many inſtances might be col‑
lected

lected from hiftory*. In fact, the operations by
fea cannot be fo mechanically and deliberately
conducted as thofe by land: the winds and tides
may lock up one fquadron, and fill the fails of
another; or a tempeft may difperfe or perhaps
deftroy the Britifh fleet, whilft the fquadrons of
their enemies are fecured in their harbours, or for-
warded by the ftorm.

Some, indeed, have endeavoured to fet forth
the idea of an invafion from France, as in itfelf
impracticable and ridiculous ; as a feint to excite
our fears, to hurt our credit, and by detaining our
forces at home to weaken our foreign exertions.
But in this cafe it is dangerous to truft too much
to plaufible theories, at leaft it is better to be de-
ceived a thoufand times over by falfe alarms, than
to be taken once unprepared.

The invaders of every country muft have three
things in view. Firft, how to get into the enemy's territories; fecondly, what oppofition they

---

* Our ableft admirals have confeffed, that a fuperiority
at fea was only a precarious defence. The Carthaginians
found fo; for with it, they could neither prevent Claudius
from getting into Sicily, nor Agathocles into Africa.
An. Un. Hift. Vol. 17, p. 443. The revolution itfelf is
an inftance how little a fleet is to be depended upon.
For if the Englifh fleet had not been prevented by contrary
winds from getting up with the Dutch one, that glorious
enterprife would have been defeated. By that accident we
then recovered our liberties, but if we fhould ever refolve
to truft entirely to our fleet, the fame accident may here-
after be the caufe of our lofing them.

D   will

will meet with there; thirdly, in the event of misfortunes, a safe retreat.

As to the first particular, it is surely unfavourable to the invaders of an island. To transport a great army by sea requires an inconceivable number both of ships and seamen*; the transports with the troops may be intercepted by the vigilance, and sometimes by the good fortune of their foes, and the invading forces destroyed on an element, where they could not expect to conquer. In their passage they may meet with storms sufficient to destroy them without the interference of a visible enemy. Or the landing in a hostile country, unless the place is very well chosen, and no opposition of any consequence given, may be found to be a very dangerous and hazardous undertaking.

But if we suppose the enemy fairly landed in England with a powerful army, unless a well-regulated militia was established, I should tremble for the event. Though our forces were as numerous as we have heard them lately represented†, yet dispersed, as they are, from one extremity of the

---

* William the Conqueror found it necessary to collect no less than 3000 vessels, great and small, for his invasion of England. Hume's Hist. Vol. 1. C. 3.

† They are generally supposed to be about 60,000 effective men, tho', perhaps, more numerous upon paper. But I question much whether 30,000 could be collected together in a month's time to act against the enemy.

island

ifland to another, we fhould find it impoffible, in a
fhort fpace of time, to collect a force ftrong
enough to cope with the enemy, and to defend
the capital, on whofe fafety this nation fo much
depends. Befides, the country is open, and we
truft fo much to our infular fituation as to have
few fortifications capable of any confiderable refiftance.

It is true, in cafe of misfortunes, that an enemy
without a great naval fuperiority could have little
chance of efcaping out of Britain; but this would
never damp the confidence of a numerous army,
trufting to its numbers, and flufhed with the profpect of plunder; nor would the dread of it prevent
their rifking an invafion; and if they once landed,
this danger would only ferve to render them def-
perate, and confequently more courageous. For
the meereft cowards have fought bravely, when
impelled by defpair*,

---

* The Englifh are never weaker, nor eafier overcome
than in their own country. Not for the reafon affigned by
Montefquieu, Spirit of Laws, l. 9, c. 8. namely, their divi-
fions at home; but from the defpair of the invader, who
muft conquer or perifh. This idea is confirmed by the arguments made ufe of by William the Conqueror to encourage his forces prior to the famous battle of Haftings:
" Inevitable deftruction, fays he, muft be the confequence
" of your difcomfiture. An enraged enemy hangs upon
" your rear, *the fea prevents your retreat*, and an ignomi-
" nious death muft be the certain punifhment of your im-
" prudence and cowardice." Hume's Hift. Vol. 1. C 3.

That

That an invafion therefore, is neither impracticable nor (in our prefent fituation at leaft) in-
capable of fuccefs, no reafonable man can deny;
and for our defence againft it, a well regulated
militia is the only fyftem to be approved of; the
only proper fource of national confidence. Other
modes are either dangerous or uncertain; that
alone, fure, uniform, and invariable. I wifh it
had fallen to the lot of fome abler hand to have
fketched out the plan of fuch a militia, fuited to
the prefent circumftances of Great Britain. 'Till
fuch a man arifes, more humble abilities muft attempt it, and however ready I may be to acknowledge myfelf inferior to others in that particular,
yet in zeal and attachment to the fervice of the
public, I will yield to none.

C H A P. II.

Of the proper System of Military Defence, for the Safety and Protection of Great Britain.

EVERY plan for a public nature muſt be varied according to the peculiar circumſtances of that nation for which it is intended; for a military ſyſtem well adapted to an inland country like Poland, or a mountainous one like Switzerland, may in ſome reſpects be but ill-ſuited to a maritime power, and an inſular ſituation. It is therefore in the firſt place neceſſary to examine, what are the peculiar circumſtances of this iſland.

It muſt ſtrike any one who ſeriouſly conſiders this ſubject, that the many diſtant and valuable territories poſſeſſed by Great Britain cannot well be defended without the aſſiſtance of regular forces. If Britain were, like Switzerland, without ſuch diſtant acquiſitions, like it, I am perſuaded, it might defend itſelf by a militia only. But when theſe poſſeſſions are taken into conſideration, the firmeſt friends to a militia muſt acknowledge, that ſome regular forces are neceſſary: and ſtill more neceſſary, if the diſtant ſettlements of our enemies were to be attacked. For no troops are ſo fit for being employed in ſuch a ſervice, as thoſe that

are

are acquainted with the fmalleft minutiæ of difcipline, and, if poffible, have been formerly inured to the field. Befides the troops neceffary for
defending our own fettlements abroad, ten thoufand foot, and five thoufand horfe, ought therefore to be always kept in England, and if any
part of them are fent away, immediately replaced
by new raifed troops, ready to be fent to any
quarter of the globe, where the interefts of Great
Britain may require it, and kept up for any fud-
den emergency, when the operation of a militia
might be found too flow and tedious.

It may in the next place be obferved, that in
time of war fome force ought always to be in
arms to defend our fhipping and dockyards, and
to be encamped for the protection of the capital.
Hence it is neceffary to have a body of men on
the footing of the prefent militia in England, but
to which the name of fencibles, or provincial
corps, may be given; which in time of peace may
be fully difciplined by being exercifed not only
every Sunday, but may be kept a month every
year in the field; and in time of war, like ftanding forces, perpetually in arms.

But as the defence of the whole kingdom, when
a proper militia is eftablifhed, will neither depend
upon regular, nor fencible, or provincial troops;
a body of thirty thoufand men, both from England and Scotland, would be as many fencibles

as would be neceſſary : twenty-four thouſand of which ought to be raiſed in England, and ſix thouſand in Scotland. Thus in time of war, an army conſiſting of forty thouſand foot and five thouſand horſe, would be perpetually in arms to aſſiſt a well regulated militia in protecting Britain in general, its coaſt and its capital. Surely then, there would be little room for apprehenſion.

Further, it ought to be conſidered, that men are at preſent permitted to ſerve in the militia by ſubſlitutes ; a regulation which ought to be imitated, if fencible troops were eſtabliſhed in their room. For to many men whoſe ſubſiſtence, and that of their families, depends upon their perſonal attention to their buſineſs, abſtracting them for a month in time of peace, and ſtill more during the whole year in time of war, might with ſome reaſon be complained of. This indulgence, too many whoſe lot it has been to ſerve in the militia have taken the benefit of ; and hence the ſoldiers of the preſent militia of England, inſtead of being men of ſubſtance, and of courſe poſſeſſing an intereſt in the ſtate abſtracted from their ſituation as ſoldiers, conſiſt of the loweſt and idleſt fellows in the kingdom. Brave they are, for that is the characteriſtic of Britons, and without doubt ſo far as their number could effect, would valiantly repel any foreign invader ; but how far they might be

brought

brought (notwithſtanding patriotic officers) to ſup-
port any domeſtick attack upon the liberties of
the country, is at beſt a diſagreeable uncertainty.
Without conſidering therefore how neceſſary it is
to have a real militia eſtabliſhed, as our beſt defence againſt foreign enemies, it ſeems alſo
neceſſary to have a number of armed and well-
diſciplined men in the kingdom: not in actual
ſervice, to make head againſt thoſe who are in
ſervice, if they ſhould ever attempt to encroach
upon the liberties of the nation. If regular forces
therefore are neceſſary to atttack our enemies
abroad, and to protect our diſtant poſſeſſions.
If fencible or provincial troops ought to be
eſtabliſhed to guard our capital, and our towns
the moſt expoſed to the inſults of the enemy : a well regulated militia is fully as neceſſary,
not only to render theſe kingdoms unconquerable
by foreign enemies, but alſo to defend the property and the privileges of the people in general
from domeſtic invaſions *.

Militias, like ſtanding armies (except in a mountainous country like Switzerland) ought to con-

* The very eſtabliſhing a proper militia would prevent
any attack upon our liberties. For a probability of ſucceſs (it has been well obſerved) is one of the greateſt in-
citements to villainy, as the contrary is the beſt preſerva-
tives of innocence.

I

fift both of horfe and foot. Indeed a numerous cavalry is the moft proper defence for an open country like England, where by quick marches it may harafs an enemy every ftep of their march. Hence the Duke of Marlborough affirmed, in the event of an invafion, that the fafety of England, would very much depend upon the multitude of its horfemen.

If both horfe and foot therefore ought to be levied; to me, it appears evident, that the firft fhould be raifed in the towns, and the fecond in the country, fo as to prevent the attention of the fame people from being diftracted by two different fervices. Befides, the inhabitants of the country, are much fitter than citizens for being foot foldiers, being more inured to labour, lefs vitiated by drink and debauchery, and abler to endure the toils and difficulties of a martial life. As the moft opulent alfo live in towns, they are better able to afford horfes proper for war, and in general they have them fo well broke, that little additional training would be neceffary to fit them for the field; whereas it would be impoffible to keep up a number of people fufficient to train the innumerable multitude of wild and ungovernable horfes fcattered through the country. Two obfervations may be added. Firft, it might be dangerous to truft every inhabitant in a populous town

E

with

with arms, particularly one fo full of people as London is, as it might endanger the peace and quiet of the nation. For the licentious inhabitants of cities are more inclined to mutiny and cabal, and may be more eafily collected for feditious purpofes, than the undebauched and fcattered inhabitants of the country. Secondly, the citizens when difciplined as a body of horfe, would check with greater facility fuch rebellious commotions as thofe of Cade and Tyler, than if trained to the exercife adapted to infantry only, and the terror of being oppofed by a numerous cavalry would probably altogether prevent fuch infurrections. A militia thus feparately and diftinctly difciplined, could never be excited by factious men to make ufe of their arms in conjunction for the difturbance of the public peace *. When difjoined, as would probably be the cafe in domeftic diforders, their force would be defective and imperfect. When united, as might always be expected againft a foreign enemy, it would be found invincible. On thefe principles the following outlines

* In Turky the fpahics and janizaries, or horfe and foot guards, are poifed and balanced againft each other. And Lord Lyttleton obferves, vol. 3. p. 92, even prior to the reign of Stephen, that the popular militia from reafons of policy was oppofed to the ariftocratical, and the forces of the towns, made a check upon thofe of the barons.

of a plan for the eftablifhment of a conftitutional
militia are founded †.

PROPOSITION I.

In the firft place it is propofed that in
every town whofe inhabitants exceed 5000
in number, (fea-port towns excepted,) a
militia of cavalry fhall be eftablifhed, and
that every inhabitant who actually keeps a
horfe or is able to maintain one, fhall be
obliged to enter himfelf into the militia of
that city, and to ferve on horfeback, either
by himfelf or a fubftitute. The fame to be
confidered as the militia of that town, and
never to be marched by the commanding
officer, above ten miles therefrom, without
an order from the magiftrates, nor above
fifteen, without an order from the crown.

As the whole body of the inhabitants are not
exercifed, and fubftitutes are allowed in oppidal
militias, none who are able to afford it, ought to
be exempted (except they have ferved for ten
years in the militia) nor any difqualified but fuch

† For fome particular articles in the following plan, and
indeed for fome of the preleminary obfervations to it, the
author is indebted to an ingenious fyftem of the fame nature, publifhed anno 1745, which however plaufible in
theory was found too intricate for practice. But that
plan itfelf is not entirely original, for in many refpects it
imitates the fyftem laid down by that great mafter of poli-
tics, Harrington.

as

as refufe to take the ufual oaths of fupremacy and
abjuration.

In towns, whofe inhabitants amount to lefs than
5000 people, no cavalry of any confequence cou'd
be raifed; confequently a militia of infantry ought
to be eftablifhed.

PROPOSITION II.

That the militia of every town fhould be
divided into two branches; light horfe and
dragoons. The firft to be formed of all fuch
as are poffeffed of 200*l.* per annum, or
4,000*l.* in money. The fecond of fuch as are
not qualified to enrol with them; as inferior
citizens, fubftitutes and the like, who may
be mounted on horfes ufed in carriages,
which are generally of a proper fize for heavy
cavalry, and may eafily be trained as dragoons.

To form a militia of light horfe of fuch as have
the greateft property in the cities, where cavalry
is eftablifhed, can be no great increafe of expence
to people of that rank, becaufe all fuch keep
horfes for health, conveniency or fhew, which with
a little attention to fize, colour and training will
anfwer all military purpofes. A uniformity in
drefs, accoutrements, and colour of horfes, ought
alfo to be attended to; (but the minute particu-

lars may be left to the tafte and fancy of the officers) for fuch circumftances, tho' in themfelves
trifling, give a more refpectable appearance to
any body of troops, make their enemies entertain
a higher notion of them, and give more confidence to their friends. Their arms, in which an
exact uniformity muft be obferved, ought to be
furnifhed at the public expence.

PROPOSITION III.

That in every county where a militia of
cavalry is eftablifhed, a grand major fhall be
appointed by the crown, with a falary from
the public, as is the cafe in Switzerland, upon
whofe requifition the magiftrate of every
town, where fuch a militia is to be raifed,
fhall make out a lift of all fuch as ought to
ferve therein, which lift fhall be tranfmitted
to the fecretary of war, and in proportion to
the numbers therein contained, colonels,
majors, captains, and other inferior officers,
fhall be appointed, by a royal commiffion,
from among the people of the greateft property in the diftrict; the captains of the fame,
and fuperior officers being entitled by fuch
commiffion to the dignity of knights.

Five thoufand light horfe, and fifteen thoufand
heavy cavalry would furely be a fufficient defence
in

in fo far as horfe is neceffary for thefe kingdoms. And as many more will be inrolled, a proportional dedu&ion may be made, according to the number that ought to be furnifhed by the different towns.

PROPOSITION IV.

That the grand major of the county fhall appoint in every town a commiffioner of arms, who fhall have a falary alfo from the public, whofe duty it is to have the horfes trained, and the whole cavalry under his charge properly exercifed, every Sunday, after public worfhip is over. The fame being reviewed by the grand major of the county, once every two months, who fhall report their ftate and progrefs in difcipline to the fecretary of war; which reports, on certain fixed days, fhall be brought under the confideration of both houfes of parliament.

PROPOSITION V.

That in every parifh where no militia of cavalry is eftablifhed, particularly in the parifhes of fea-port towns which are moft expofed to invafion, the officiating clergyman and church-wardens, upon an order and requifition from the lord lieutenant of the county,

ty, fhall tranfmit to him a lift of all perfons
from eighteen to fifty, capable of bearing
arms, in proportion to whofe numbers, captains and other officers fhall be appointed by
the lord lieutenant from among fuch as refide
in the parifh, and have the moft confiderable
property therein; which militia fhall never
be obliged to march out of the parifh, without an order from the lord lieutenant, nor
out of he county without an order from the
crown.

As no fubftitutes are allowed in the infantry militia, perfons coming under the following defcription ought to be exempted : the clergy, peers,
and members of parliament ; the judges, officers
of the houfhold, treafury, exchequer ; admiralty
and navy boards ; all counfellors at law, &c.
during the terms and affizes ; phyficians, furgeons,
and the like ; and fuch as are incapacitated by age
or bodily infirmities.

PROPOSITION VI.

That the commanding officer, or fenior
captain in every parifh, fhall appoint a parifh
corporal, who has been in the army, and is
well acquainted with military difcipline, who
fhall have a falary alfo from the public, and
the charge of the parochial arms and ammunition

nition given him, and whofe duty it fhall be to train the militia of the parifh, every Sunday, in the ufual exercifes of the foot.

PROPOSITION VII.

That the lord lieutenant fhall have the command of the infantry militia in the county, with the power of nominating the field officers in the refpective hundreds, who fhall affemble the regimented militia of the hundred for three days in time of peace, and fix days in time of war, to be exercifed together, and in the event of any imminent danger of an invafion from abroad, may encamp them for a fortnight in the month of May or June, to render their difcipline more complete, during which periods they fhall receive pay from the public. Their progrefs in difcipline to be from time to time reported by the lord lieutenant to the fecretary at war, for parliamentary difcuffion, which muft prevent fuch a fyftem falling into decay, unlefs every fpark of Britifh patriotifm fhould be extinguifhed.

The infantry militia ought to be divided into two claffes; the firft, confifting of the unmarried; the fecond, of all the married men in the diftrict. The firft, or unmarried clafs, ought to be regimented, and always ready to march upon the

fhorteft

fhorteft notice. The fecond clafs ought never to be drawn from home, except in the event of an actual invafion, or imminent danger of it.

PROPOSITION VIII.

That military difcipline fhall only be enforced in fuch a militia by pecuniary fines or perfonal confinement. The parochial officers may conftitute a court martial, and fine to the amount of five pounds, or imprifon for five days. If a greater punifhment is thought neceffary for the offence, a court martial of the hundred may be appointed for trying the offender, whofe powers, as alfo thofe of oppidal courts martial, fhall extend to two months imprifonment, and twenty pounds of fine. Such as behave well ought to be gratified by fome pecuniary reward, or confpicuous mark of diftinction.

PROPOSITION IX.

That thofe who neglect or refufe to obey the regulations enacted for the eftablifhment of a national militia, fhall be punifhed as follows: firft, if the lord lieutenant of any county, the magiftrates of any town, or the minifters and church-wardens of any parifh fhall neglect or refufe to carry the above re-

F   gulations,

gulations, in fo far as depends upon them,
into execution, they fhall forfeit their refpective offices and employments, and new ones
may be chofen or appointed. Secondly, for
the punifhment of other offenders, the following fines and penalties are propofed:

TABLE of MILITARY FINES and TAXES.

Tax per annum on fuch as refufe the
oaths of fupremacy or allegiance, or
have neglected to enter themfelves
into the light horfe after being le-
gally inrolled

	l.	*s.*	*d.*
Tax ... gally inrolled	25	0	0
Ditto, if in the dragoons,	10	10	0
Ditto, if in the infantry,	5	5	0
Fine to be paid by the field-officers of the cavalry, if they refufe to act,	30	0	0
Ditto, if in the infantry,	25	0	0
Ditto, if captains in the cavalry,	20	0	0
Ditto, if captains in the infantry,	15	15	0
Ditto, if fubalterns in the cavalry,	12	12	0
Ditto, if fubalterns in the infantry,	8	8	0

Other fines for deferting the fervice without
caufe, &c. to depend upon the parochial and oppidal courts martial, confifting of all the officers
of the refpective diftricts. Such fines to be levied on the goods and chattels of the delinquents,
by a warrant from the commanding officer in the
city

tity or parifh, figned by two of his Majefty's juf-
tices of the peace, and put into execution by fuch
conftable or other petty officer as they may direct
it to. Such fines, after deducting one fhilling
per pound for his trouble, fhall be paid by the
conftable to the commanding officer who granted
the warrant, for which he fhall be accountable.
The fums levied by fines and taxes in the firft
place to be applied for paying the general expences
of the militia, and the balance to be at the dif-
pofal of the refpective courts martial in whofe diftrict they are raifed, and to be expended in providing drums, butts for fhooting at, and other military purpofes.

PROPOSITION. X.

That in every town where a militia of cavalry is eftablifhed, as alfo in fea-port towns,
a certain body of men, in proportion to the
number of its inhabitants, fhall be taught all
the arts of engineering by firing of cannons and
mortars, at butts erected for that fpecial purpofe; the ammunition, &c. to be provided
at the public expence.

On two accounts, the artillery ought to be confined to towns; firft, to accuftom the cavalry to
the noife of cannon, which would render the horfe
fitter for real action; and fecondly, to be a far-

F 2   ther

ther check upon the militia of the country, who could never expect to be fuccefsful in any feditious infurrection, if oppofed both by horfe and artillery, and without having either to fupport them.

In thefe ten propofitions, the general outline of the plan is comprifed. Many additional regulations might be fuggefled, but it feems unneceffary to enter into the more minute particulars, unlefs the general fyftem is approved of.

On the fyftem of national defence above propofed, it may in the firft place be remarked, that if it were carried into execution, no foreign power could ever fubjugate Great Britain unlefs we were dif-united at home, or unlefs Providence interfered in behalf of our enemies. We fhould in that cafe in time of war, have a ftanding force of 40,000 foot and 5000 horfe, and a militia at leaft amounting to 600,000 infantry, and 20,000 cavalry*, a force fufficient to fubdue the world, inftead of being only fit to defend fuch an inconfiderable part of it.

Befides, fuch a defence whilft it was more fecure, would alfo prove much lefs expenfive than the prefent fyftem. By it, the pay of fome part of the

* In the year 1583, there was a general review made of all the men in England capable of bearing arms, and they were found to amount to about 1,200,000. Hume's Hift. appendix to chap. 50. Both in England and Scotland then; 600,000 infantry may be reckoned upon at this time (exclufive of towns) even in the country.

militia

militia on the prefent fyftem, and of many regiments of regular forces would be faved to the public. Inftead of which, if the arms were once provided, fcarcely any additional expence would be neceffary. For the grand majors, the commiffioners of arms, and the parifh corporals, would fave the half-pay lift, and the revenues of Chelfea Hofpital; and the fines and taxes above propofed would probably raife a fum equal to any farther expence, without encroaching upon the public revenue. But fuppofing that the expence of a general militia amounted to 200,000£ per annum; how trifling will it appear, in comparifon of the enormous fums at prefent lavifhed for the national protection.

Nor can any plan of a general military eftablifhment be contrived lefs deftructive to induftry. The people are exercifed on that day of the week only, when they muft be idle, nay, in towns where manufactures are eftablifhed, none but the opulent are trained to arms; fo that a flothful fpirit will never be excited among the induftrious part of the nation: at any rate to fpend a part of every Sunday in military exercifes cannot have a worfe effect upon the induftry of a mechanic, than fpending the whole of it, as is too frequently the cafe at prefent, in idlenefs and debauchery*.

* The late alderman Beckford obferved in the lower houfe, that a part of every Sunday would be much better fpent

Such a military fyftem alfo muft prove highly
favourable to liberty; firft, by diminifhing the
numbers or at leaft removing the neceffity of a great
ftanding army; and, fecondly, by putting the
fword (where it ought to be) in the hands of the
peop'e, without which, no limitation of monarchy
can give any real fecurity to the privileges of
fubjects. Indeed when the people are unarmed
and undifciplined they may with impunity be op-
preffed by the king, fupported by a ftanding army.
Refiftance (with the army againft them); only
ferves to rivet their chains, or to haften on the fad
hour of defpotifm; nor can any nation pretend to
be free, when the only men in arms are under the
fole command and confequently at the devotion of
the crown. He who wields the fword of the ftate,
muft have its purfe at his mercy: and Charles the
Firft might impute his want of fuccefs to this,
that he attempted to open the one, before he had
grafped the other.

Moreover, fuch a militia will not be deficient
in valor. In fact, men in northern climates, (particularly where the government is a free one) are
naturally brave, and the great art of defpotifm is
to fubdue their natural courage, and to render

spent in learning to defend one's country, than in fitting
at the alehoufe, or fauntering in the fields, as moft of the
common people do at prefent. Lord Talbot fupported
fimilar fentiments in the upper affembly.

them

them timid and fearful. God forbid that such
baneful arts fhould ever prove fuccefsful in Britain.

Nor would fuch a militia be in any way defective
in the effential article of difcipline. For a knowledge
of military exercifes fufficient for national defence
is far from being fo difficult to acquire as is generally imagined. Nor does it require any extra-
ordinary exertions in the fovereign, to preferve or
to excite a martial fpirit almoft in any nation *.
To their officers likewife, all due obedience may
be expected: they are once a week under the military command of thofe, who are the moft opulent and refpectable people in the diftrict, and confequently muft enjoy a confiderable fhare of civil
influence and authority over them. Nay, fuch a
militia muft be more inclined to obey their commanders, than the foldiers of a ftanding army,
whofe officers are frequently changing their corps,
and varying their ranks, and alfo frequently abfent
from their refpective regiments for a confiderable
length of time.

It would likewife be of the utmoft confequence
to have fuch a plan carried into execution, if it

* So ftrong is the natural profperity of men towards
military fhows and exercifes, that little attention in the
fovereign is fufficient to excite and fupport a martial fpirit
in a nation: at leaft the Englifh found fo, when under the
dominion of that pacific monarch James the Firft. Hume's
Hift. of England, appendix to chap. 50.

were

were only for the fake of eſtabliſhing a ſyſtem of ſubordination and order in the event of an inva-ſion. Without order, ſays the gallant Sidney, no numbers of men, however valiant, are able to defend themſelves. Their multitude breeds con-fuſion.—Their wealth, when it is like to be made a prey of, increaſes the fears of the owners, and the ſpirits of the enemy. And they, who, if they were brought into good order, might conquer a great part of the world, (being deſtitute of that advantage), dare not think of defending them-ſelves.

Laſtly, ſuch a plan might be carried into exe-cution with but very little difficulty, and with little additional loſs of time, or inconvenience to individuals, than that to which they are at pre-ſent ſubjected. In times of ſuch public danger, every one would moſt aſſuredly exert himſelf. If Grand Majors were appointed, ſkilful in military affairs, the cavalry would ſoon be brought into ſome kind of order, and fit for many eſſential pur-poſes in the event of an invaſion. If an inhabi-tant of every pariſh in England, now in the mi-litia, were diſmiſſed, there would be abundance of pariſh corporals to train the infantry, and ac-tive Lord Lieutenants would ſoon effect their be-ing fully diſciplined. Nay in caſe of imminent danger, they might be exerciſed oftener than once a-week. To conclude, in the words of a ſpirited

anonymous

anonymous writer, if to free our country from the continual dread of invafion; to leffen the neceffity of maintaining large ftanding armies in time of peace, or relying on troops raw, and perfectly undifciplined on the emerging of a war, if to revive that ancient military fpirit, formerly fo prevalent in the nation; and to train ourfelves to the exercifes of war, for the defence of our country: if thefe are objects of any national importance, it becomes every individual, actuated by the leaft fpark of patriotifm, to exert his utmoft influence to procure the eftablifhment of fuch a militia, as may be found the moft likely to effectuate fuch great and important purpofes.

G   C H A P.

C H A P. III.

*Observations on the Plan lately proposed for arming
the Towns, with some Thoughts on the Propriety of
exercising the Militia on Sunday.*

THE plan lately proposed by one of his
Majesty's principal Secretary's of State,
having occasioned much speculation, it may not
be improper to make a few short observations
upon it, and in particular upon the regulation it
proposes, of exercising the militia on the Sabbath-
day. The plan to which I allude, as submitted
to the consideration of the public, was conceived
in the following terms :

HEADS *of a* PLAN *for raising Corps in several
principal Towns in Great-Britain.*

1st. The principal towns in Great-Britain to
furnish one or more battalions each, or a certain
number of companies each, in proportion to their
size and number of inhabitants.

2d. The officers to be appointed from among
the gentlemen of the neighbourhood, or the inhabitants of the said towns, either by commission
from his Majesty, or from the Lord Lieutenant
of the county, upon the recommendation of the

chief

chief magiftrate of the town in which the corps are raifed.

3d. They are to be poffeffed of fome certain eftate in land or money, in proportion to their rank:

4th. An adjutant or town major in each town to be appointed by his Majefty.

5th. A proper number of ferjeants and corporals from the army to be appointed for the corps in each town, in proportion to their numbers.

6th. The faid ferjeants and corporals, as well as the adjutant, or town major, to be in the government pay.

7th. The men to exercife frequently, either in battalions, or by companies, on Sundays, and on all holidays, and alfo after their work is over in the evenings.

8th. Arms, accoutrements, and ammunition, to be furnifhed at the expence of government, if required.

9th. Proper magazines, or ftorehoufes, to be chofen, or erected in each town, for keeping the faid arms, &c.

10th. The arms and accoutrements to be delivered out at times of exercife only, and to be returned into the ftorehoufes as foon as the exercife is finifhed.

11th. The adjutant, or town major, to be always prefent at exercife, and to fee that the men

after-

aftewards march regularly, and lodge their arms in the ftorehoufes.

12th. Proper penalties to be inflicted on fuch as abfent themfelves from exercife, as alfo for difobedience of orders, infolence to their officers, and other diforderly behaviour.

13th. The above corps not to be obliged, on any account, or by any authority whatever to move from their refpective towns, except in time of actual invafion or rebellion.

14th. His Majefty fhall then have power to order the faid corps to march to any part of Great-Britain, as his fervice may require.

15th. They are on fuch occafions to act either feparately, or in conjuction with his Majefty's regular forces, and be under the command of fuch general officers as his Majefty fhall think proper to appoint.

16th. Both officers and men to receive full pay as his Majefty's other regiments of foot, from the day of their march, and as long as they fhall continue on fervice out of their towns.

17th. They are to be fubject to military difcipline, in the fame manner as his Majefty's regular forces, during the faid time of their being fo called out, and receiving government's pay.

18. All officers who fhould be difabled in actual fervice to be entitled to half pay, and all

non-

non-commiſſioned officers and private men diſ-
abled, to receive the benefit of Chelſea hoſpital.

19th. The widows of officers killed in the
ſervice to have a penſion for life *.

---

* Theſe propoſitions were accompanied with the following letter, which does infinite honour to the patriotiſm
and public ſpirit of the noble lord, by whom it its ſub-
ſcribed.

Whitehall, 7th of May, 1782.

C I R C U L A R   C O P Y.

S I R,

His Majeſty has commanded me to expreſs his firm re-
liance upon the ſpirit and loyalty of his people, and his
royal confidence, that, during this ſeaſon of difficulty,
their utmoſt endeavours will not be wanting to give un-
queſtionable proofs of their attachment and emulation
for his ſervice; and foreſeeing, that by wiſe, ſtrenuous,
and timely preparations, he may not only diſappoint, or
defeat any hoſtile attempts, but, by appearing ſtrong and
united at home, he may be enabled to make the more
powerful efforts for maintaining his honour and the public
intereſts abroad, and thereby lay the ſureſt foundations for
a ſafe, an honorable, and a laſting peace; and as the po-
pulouſneſs of the principal towns and cities of Great-Britain, naturally offers the greateſt facility, as well for form-
ing into corps, as for learning the military exerciſe, without loſs of time, interruption of labour, or any conſidera-
ble fatigue, His Majeſty has commanded me to tranſmit to
you the encloſed propoſition, which has been ſubmitted
to His Majeſty, as at leaſt a temporary plan for augment-
ing the domeſtic force of the nation, which being adopted
or improved, according to the circumſtances and ſituation
of the town, of which you are the chief magiſtrate, may
tend to the immediate formation of a great and reſpectable
addition to the national force at home, on the moſt natural
and conſtitutional principles.

For

This plan, at leaft as a general fyftem of national defence, feems to be defective; in the firft
place as containing no provifion for the eftablifhment of a militia of cavalry, without which this
ifland cannot be fafe from the invafions of its enemies. Enough has been faid in the preceding
chapter on the neceffity of having a large body of
horfe, and of the propriety of raifing them in the
towns; and the London Horfe Affociation fully
proves what might be done in the capital, if that
fpirit were properly encouraged*.

The noble Lord's fyftem in the next place is
exceptionable, on account of its propofing to arm
the towns, whilft it leaves the inhabitants of the
country, who are much better calculated to act as

For this purpofe, I have His Majefty's commands to fig-
nify to you his defire and recommendation, that you fhould
take the fame into immediate confideration, and, after
having confidered, report to me whatever obfervations may
occur to you for the carrying into execution a plan, the
purpofe of which is to give fecurity to your own perfons
and property, and to the general defence of the kingdom.

I am, Sir,
Your moft obedient
Humble fervant,
(Signed)   SHELBURNE.

* It has often occurred to me, that the races of New-
market, and other places in the kingdom, might be con-
verted to beneficial military purpofes, by obliging every
perfon who attends fuch meetings, to have a horfe trained,
either for the light horfe or the dragoons, and to be exercifed during the race week. Thus what is at prefent a
misfortune to the country, might become an addition to
its fecurity, and to its ftrength.

foldiers,

foldiers, in a manner unarmed and defenceless. Not to mention that arming the country cannot prove fatal to induſtry, whereas it will be very difficult to make the ſame individual an active ſoldier and an induſtrious mechanic†.

Beſides, without entering into more minute objections‡, it may be remarked, that arming any large body of people, who live contiguous to each other, is at beſt a dangerous experiment, and would probably be repented of, if the people thought they had any reaſon to be diſſatisfied with their rulers, on account of any partial ſtagnation of trade, or any temporary ſcarcity of proviſions, and ſtill more if their paſſions were enflamed, by the envenomed harangues of any popular demagogue.

Laſtly, it appears to me that the inhabitants of the country might be fully as well trained to the

---

† It is well known how much the two warlike nations of Rome and Sparta, deſpiſed the military aſſiſtance of artiſans.

‡ The ſecond propoſition, by which the officers of the different corps are to be recommended by the chief magiſtrate of the town in which the corps is raiſed, from among the gentlemen of the neighbourhood, ſeems to place the magiſtrate of the towns in a rank ſuperior to the gentlemen of the country. The 14th propoſition alſo appears to be exceptionable; for in the event of an actual invaſion the people would voluntarily turn out: and he who has not ſpirit enough to march, of his own accord, when an enemy has landed, had much better be left at home.

exerciſes

exercifes of war on Sundays and other holidays, as the citizens of towns; and that if they are regularly affembled once a week, it is as frequent an intercoufe with each other, and perhaps in as large a body as ought to be permitted to the foldiers of any militia, not ftrictly difciplined. This leads me, however, to juftify the fyftem of training a militia on the Sabbath-day, on the propriety of which the decifion of any controverfy on this fubject, muft in a great meafure depend.

Among the Jews, from whom that wife inftitution was taken, the Sabbath was far from being ftrictly kept in military matters, even during the beft period of their exiftence as a nation. The taking of Jericho itfelf was effected on a Sabbath-day, one of the firft warlike enterpifes after the law was promulgated, undertaken by the fpecial direction, and perfected by the powerful influence of heaven itfelf[*]. On the fame day we are alfo informed, that Jonathan took his bow and arrows, and under pretence of fhooting, gave David notice of Saul's intention againft his life, which he could not have done without fufpicion, had not the Sabbath been a common day with them, for the arts and the exercifes of war[†].

* Heylin on the Sabbath, 1. 6. § 5.
† 1 Sam. xx. 35. This event happened on a day when the old fhew bread was taken away, and frefh bread put in its ftead, which was only done on Sabbath-days. 1 Sam. xxi.

With refpect to the principles and the practice
of Chriftians in military affairs, there is every reafon to believe that warlike exercifes were as lawful
to them as they could be to other people. In
fcripture we find no anti-military commands; and
Tertullian informs us, " Quod non prohibetur,
permiffum eft." To defend ourfelves is our right
by nature, whofe laws the Chriftian religion was
never intended to deftroy. John the Baptift, inftead of abrogating war, permitted foldiers to continue in their military profeffion*. And, in the
words of our Saviour, a greater prophet than he
was never born of woman†. Chrift himfelf permitted his difciples to purchafe arms ‡, how then
can the ufing them be unlawful? The firft Gentile
that was baptized was a Centurion§; nor does it
appear that he was enjoined to lay down his arms,
or to quit his military employments. Private re-
venge, or war among individuals, it is true, is
frequently condemned in the gofpel; but the taking up arms in the defence of one's country by
the direction of a magiftrate, whofe orders we are

xxi. 6. On a Sabbath-day alfo, Ahab defeated the Sy-
rians with great flaughter. 1 Kings xx. 29.
* Luke iii. 14.
† Luke vii. 28.
‡ Nay, it is faid, " He that hath no fword, let him fell
his garment and buy one." Luke xxii. 36.
§ Acts x. 2. and xi. 1.

commanded to obey *, none but enthufiafts can boggle at.

Among the primitive Chriftians 'tis true, fome men avoided places of authority and power, and were not fond of engaging in military matters; but as Cave obfervest†, this was only the opinion of fome private individuals, and not the general practice, nor fupported by the authority of the church. The victory obtained by Marcus Antoninus over the Quadi and Marcomanni is imputed to the valour as well as to the prayers of his Chriftian Soldiers‡.

When Maximinian was fent to Gaul to fupprefs a dangerous rebellion there, he took with him a band of Chriftians, confifting of 6666 men, remarkable for their valour and difcipline§. Julian's army was almoft wholly compofed of Chriftians, nor did his foldiers refufe to obey any orders given them, when they were not urged to idolatry‖.

* Romans xiii. 1. Titus iii. 1. and 1 Peter ii. 13.
† Cave's Primitive Chriftianity, p. 34.
‡ Cave, p. 58. Addifon's Remarks in his Travels, p. 206, &c. There is great reafon to believe, from certain medals and infcriptions on Antonine's pillar, from Julius Capitolinus's hiftory, and Claudean's poems, that this ftory is not without foundation.
§ Though fome authors deny *the martyrdom of* the Thebean Legion. Vide Gibbon's hiftory, vol. 1. p. 566. Vindic. p. 121. Yet that fuch a body of Chriftians were actually in arms is highly probable.
‖ Cave, p. 72.

Nor in military matters was there ever any peculiar deference shown to the sanctity of the Lord's-day; for Justinian enacted, that what pertained to military discipline should not be neglected on any of the festivals observed by Christians*. Indeed the prohibition of avoiding to do any manner of work on the seventh day, could not be extended to warlike affairs, unless Christians were bound to observe the sabbath with a more than Jewish rigour and austerity.

Both in England and on the Continent, many battles are recorded in history to have been fought on Sunday†. Heylin, with great reason, infers from a canon of the council of Carthage, held anno 398, that shooting and other manly exercises were permitted‡. The citizens of Geneva were, of old, accustomed to exercise themselves in shooting with crofs bows, and the like, on the Lord's Day; neither did the clergy find fault therewith, so that none were hindered from hearing the word of God at the time appointed§.

Nor was Sunday formerly in England solely dedicated to religious duties; on the contrary, in the

* Digeft. 2. 12. § 9.
† Charles Mortel defeated Hilpericus. King of France, on Palm Sunday, anno 1718. The famous battle of Lincoln, anno 1142, in which Stephen was taken prisoner, was fought on a Sunday. Many other instances occur in history.
‡ Heylin on the Sabbath, 2. 6. § 9.
§ Heylin, 2. 6. § 9.

reign

reign of Henry the Second we are informed, that companies of young men were accuftomed on Sunday, after dinner, to ride out into the fields on horfes fit for war, and the citizens of London were wont to iffue out through the gates by troops, furnifhed with lances and warlike fhields, where they made a reprefentation of battle, exercife, and fkirmifh, and many reforted there who had not as yet attained to the warlike girdle, to train and fkirmifh‡. Upon the holidays alfo, during the fummer, the youth were exercifed in leaping, fhooting, wreftling, cafting of ftones, throwing of javelines, and other military exercifes. Thus our anceftors were accuftomed to fpend their Sundays and other holidays; and thus that brave militia was formed that fought at Creffey, and at Agincourt, and remained conquerors in the bloody field of Poicticrs.

Nay, military exercifes on Sundays, at different times, have been fpecially enjoined by parliamentary authority. For by 12 Ric. 2. c. 6. it was enacted, " That all fervants and labourers fhall " have bows and arrows, *and ufe the fame on Sun-* " *days and other holidays*"; and the fheriffs, mayors, bailiffs, and conftables, had power given them to arreft all doers againft that ftatute.

‡ Extract from William Fitz Stephen's defcription of London, prefixed to the life of Becket. Vide alfo Annual Regifter, vol. 7. p. 182, and Lord Lyttleton's Hift. 3 Edit. vol. 3. p. 60.

Which

Which act was afterwards confirmed, by 11 Henry IV. c. 4, and ordered to be firmly holden and kept in all time coming. By a declaration of James the Ift. anno 1618, repeated by Charles his fon, it was determined that *archery*, vaulting, leaping, and other manly exercifes on the Lord's-day were not unlawful; and the Scotch militia was formerly exercifed on Sundays and other holidays, and butts were erected for that fpecial purpofe in the neighbourhood of churches *.

Nor ought it to be omitted, that when the prefent militia was eftablifhed, the fame principles were adopted. The firft bill that paffed the Houfe of Commons; enacted, that the militia fhould be exercifed on Sunday, tho' in confequence of the oppofition given it by the Diffenters, that claufe was afterwards dropt. The whole bill had met with fo many obftructions in its progrefs, from the ignorance and political prejudices of many, that our fenators were refolved to give no man an opportunity of objecting to it on the fcore of religion.

The oppofition therefore given by the Diffenters, to the claufe for exercifing the militia on Sunday, is the more to be wondered at, both becaufe it was the ancient method of difciplining the militia in their own country, and as in other Pro-

* 1 James 1. c. 18.---6 James 5. c. 91. In the general name holidays, Sunday was then included.

teftant,

teftant, nay Calviniftical ftates, fimilar regulations
at that very time were carried into execution,
without any danger to religion *. Indeed to qua-
lify one's felf on any day to defend our country
can have nothing contrary to the pureft fyftem of
religion. It has not in view, conqueft, and de-
vaftation, revolutions in ftates and empires, and
the deftruction of the fpecies, but only public and
private defence. If it is lawful to do well on the
fabbath, as our Saviour informs us, furely nothing
better can be done on any day, than to fit ourfelves
for refifting tyranny and oppreffion. If works of
neceffity and mercy only are permitted ; what can
be more neceffary than to be always prepared to
defend ourfelves, our families, and our country ?

Nay, to prepare ourfelves for the defence of
our religious as well as civil liberties, may be
confidered to be a moft important and neceffary
branch of our duty as Chriftians. Such a prepa-
ration ought to be accounted a pious and devout
exercife, perfectly fit to be practifed on the Lord's
Day. By thus employing a part of that time
which at prefent is too often fpent in idlenefs and
debauchery, the youth will be prevented from
heedleffly running into many dangerous and per-

* Geneva, the mother of Prefbyterian churches, at
that very time exercifed its militia on Sunday, without
any detriment to religion. And the practice is ftill general
in Switzerland.

nicious

nicious vices. Military exercises, says, an ingenious author, can never be judged a profanation
of the day set apart for religious purposes; since
self preservation is the first law of God, given as
well for the defence of nations, as of each individual, and not to be exercised in any way so ef-
fectually as by military discipline. Is not that
exercise fully as innocent as any of those amuse-
ments generally permitted on the sabbath, much
more conducive to the public good, and to the
preservation of the Proteſtant religion, *againſt the
open aſſaults of Popery?* Perhaps a better means
cannot be devised, to fruſtrate even the secret
machinations of Jesuitical Miſſionaries in the work
of conversion, than by making it the duty of all
the common people to attend public worship on
Sunday, when they may be inſtructed both in the
true principles of the Proteſtant religion, and in
the arts of discipline by which alone it can be defended against a powerful and begotted adver-
sary*. This argument, if every other proved in-
effectual, must surely have no small degree of
influence on our brethren of the North, who have
lately shewn such a stern abhorrence of Roman
Catholic intrusion.

To conclude, the proper idea of a sabbath or
weekly festival for Chriſtians to adopt, is, a day
dedicated to God and to the public. A day ap-

* Plan of a national militia. Part I. Introduction.

propriated

propriated to cultivate the principles of religion, to encourage a spirit of induſtry, and to propagate a knowledge of the art of diſcipline among the people. For theſe are the three things which the rulers of a free ſtate ought to promote among thoſe they govern.

The firſt is neceſſary to make them virtuous, without which they can neither love their God, nor their neighbour, nor have a regard to the ſociety they belong to. The ſecond is neceſſary to make them rich, without which they cannot enjoy the comforts and conveniencies of this life, in any tolerable degree of perfection; and the third is requiſite to make them brave, for men without courage are ruled by fear, and can neither defend their wealth, their liberty, nor their religious principles againſt a daring invader.

The firſt may be done, by joining in worſhiping the ſame deity, by liſtning to the ſame obſervations, to explain our duty, and the ſame exhortations to practiſe it. The ſecond, by rewarding thoſe who have been induſtrious, and publickly reproving the idle. And the third may eaſily be effected by appropriating a certain part of the Sabbath-day to the exerciſes of war.

CHAP,

CHAP. IV.

Confiderations on a Scotch Militia.

IT will be proper to begin the inveftigation of
this fubject by a general review of the laws
which have been enacted, and the regulations
which are now in force, refpecting a Scotch militia.

Perhaps no legiflature ever took more pains to
incite, and to preferve a military fpirit, than the
parliament of Scotland. It obliged every individual in the kingdom, in proportion to his rank
and fortune, to have certain kinds of arms in
his poffeffion *; and at certain ftated periods to
produce them to the public †. It encouraged the
fabrication of fuch arms in the kingdom ‡, and
the importation of them from foreign countries §.
It enacted, that on Sundays and other holidays ‖,
every man fhould be trained in the arts and exercifes of war, under the direction of fome able

---

* 9 Jac. 1. c. 120, 121, 122, 123. 11 Jac 3. c. 80.
† 2 Jac. 1. c. 44. 3 Jac. 1. c. 60. 14 Jac. 2. c. 64.
6 Jac. 3. c. 44. 3 Jac. 4. c. 31. 6 Jac. 4. c. 75. 6 Jac. 5.
c. 85, 86, 87, 88, 89. 90.
‡ 11 Jac. 3. c. 80.
§ 7 Jac. 5. c. 95.
‖ Sunday was then included in the general term of ho-
liday.

I   officer,

officer, called the captain of the parish*. Nay, the feeds of a standing army, were laid by raising a small body of men, whose sole duty was to attend as a guard, on the person of their sovereign †.

In the reign of Charles the Second, however, the Scotish legislature was not satisfied with general regulations. Experience had fully proved to them, (during their contests with the Protector of England,) that it was necessary to have a certain body of men peculiarly dedicated to the exercises of war, otherwise they could not resist the firm attacks of a veteran army. It was therefore enacted, by a bill which passed anno 1672, intitled an Act for settling the Militia; that 20,000 foot, and 2000 horse, should be raised by proportions, in the different shires of the kingdom, to be always in readiness for the service of their sovereign, whenever their assistance was demanded ‡. Nay, in addition to this force, to

---

* 1 Jac. 1. c. 18. 6 Jac. 5. c. 91.

† 8 Jac. 6. c. 137. This guard consisted of only forty gentlemen; but every one knows, that the enormous standing army of France sprung from almost as despicable an original.

‡ 1 Car. 2. sess. 3. c. 26. 2 Car. 2. c. 2. 2 Car. 2. sess. 3. c. 1. This body of men greatly resembled the present militia of England. Their establishment occasioned much jealousy in the southern part of the island; for, by the acts above-mentioned, the King was empowered to send them to England, or even to Ireland, if he judged it proper or necessary.

which

which the name of *militia* was given: the parliament farther declared, " That the kingdom would
" be ready, every man betwixt fixteen and fixty,
" to join and hazard their lives and fortunes, as
" they fhall be called for, by His Majefty, for
" the fafety and prefervation of his facred perfon,
" authority, and government *."

Laftly, by the famous Act, for the fecurity of the kingdom, paffed anno 1704, it was ordained,
" That the whole Proteftant heritors, and all the
" boroughs within the kingdom, fhall forthwith
" provide themfelves with fire arms for all the
" *fencible* men who are Proteftants, within their
" refpective bounds, and the faid heritors and
" boroughs, are hereby impowered and ordained
" to difcipline and exercife their faid fencible men,
" once in a month at leaft. The faid heritors al-
" ways taking the oaths of allegiance and affu-
" rance, before the fheriff of the fhire, or any
" other judge, within whofe jurifdiction they re-
" fide §."

<hr/>

* 1 Car. 2. c. 26. The acts in the reign of King William, refpecting national defence (acts of convention, c. 11. 20, 23, 24. 1 W. c. 7. 1 W. feff. 5. c. 33. 1 W. feff. 6. c. 23.) contain nothing remarkable, except a fingular agreement between the King and the Parliament of Scotland, by which, in confideration of an annual fupply of 1000 recruits, the militia of the country were not to be raifed, except in the event of an actual invafion.

§ The above claufe, in the Act of Security, was fufpended by 1 Anne, feff. 4. c. 3, and c. 10. until the firft day of January 1708; afterwards by 1 Geo. 1. c. 54.

The

Thus it appears, that by the law of Scotland, as it now ftands, it is in the King's power to levy a militia of 20,000 foot, and 2,000 horfe in that country, to be fent to any part af his Britifh dominions that he may think proper. That he is alfo intitled to demand the fervice of every individual from fixteen to fixty; nay, farther, that every proteftant in Scotland is at this moment impowered to have fire arms in his poffeffion, and may be trained at leaft once a month in the exercifes of war. Having thus ftated how the law exifts with refpect to this fubject, I fhall next examine how far it is proper and neceffary to alter or amend, at this particular period, thefe ancient regulations.

After the act of 1663, the military ftrength of Scotland, was of two kinds, fencibles and militia; to which, fince its union with England, ftanding forces may be added.

The inhabitants of the fhires, north of Leven in Dumbartonfhire, and of Forth in Stirlingfhire, were difarmed, which was continued by 11 Geo. 1. c. 26. for feven years longer, and from thence to the end of the then next feffion of parliament. Thefe regulations were renewed by 19 Geo. 2. c. 39. 21 Geo. 2. c. 34. and 26 Geo. 2. c. 29. by which laft act, the difarming laws were continued for feven years, from the firft of Auguft, 1753, and from thence to the end of the then next feffion of parliament; confequently they expired on the 19th day of March, 1761. The acts as to the highland drefs, 19 Geo. 2. c. 39. 20 G. 2. c. 51. and 21 Geo. 2. c. 33. not being limited in their duration, ftill remain in full force.

The

The fencibles did not, as at prefent, confift of a limited body of men, raifed by any powerful lord in a particular diftrict; but they comprehended, in the words of an old act of parliament, " Every man, able of perfon, to bear arms," in every county of the kingdom*. Under proper reftric-tions, it is evident that every individual in a free ftate ought to be trained to the ule of arms. But having already given an opinion upon that fubject it may be only neceffary to add, that to eftablifh a durable and permanent inftitution of that nature, is attended with greater difficulties than at firft fight one is apt to imagine. It is therefore proba-ble that fuch a fcheme will not be attempted with-out ferious confideration, nor until the nation at large has had fufficient time to beftow upon it mature deliberation. That fhould not, however, prevent arms being diftributed in any diftrict pe-culiarly expofed to the attacks of an enemy.

* 6 Jac. 5. c. 86. The diftinction between the fencibles and the militia, particularly appears from the 11th act of the convention of eftates, 30th March, 1689; it is inti-tled, " A Proclamation for calling together the Militia on " this fide Tay, and the Fencible Men in fome Shires." In that act there is a claufe, " That whereas there is no " militia foot in the fhires of Lanerk, Air, &c. therefore " power is granted to the commiffioners of militia, to " bring together all the fencible men in their refpective " fhires, and to model them into companies, &c. In the book intitled, " An Account of the Proceedings of the " Parliament of Scotland, which met at Edinburgh, May " 6, 1703," there is, page 226, a fimilar definition of fencible men.

But

But the queſtion for our conſideration at pre-
ſent is, whether Scotland ought to have what has
been called *a miltia* both in that country and in
England; or, in other words, a *body of men collected from all the different diſtricts in the kingdom,
ſerving by rotation, peculiarly appropriated for internal
defence, and not totally ſubjected (except in times of
imminent danger) to the duties of a ſoldier.*

Many are the advantages attending ſuch an inſtitution.

By eſtabliſhing a body of men who are never to
be ſent out of the kingdom, officers may acquire a
certain degree of military knowledge and experience, who would never think of enliſting into a
ſtanding army, or would not chuſe to run the riſk
of being ſent to contend with the frigid regions of
Canada, or the ſultry climes of Indoſtan.

By collecting ſuch a corps from every diſtrict in
the kingdom, a military ſpirit is not confined to
any particular ſpot, but is proportionally extended
throughout every corner of the country.

By compelling every individual to ſerve by rotation, as a ſoldier for the ſtate, the duties of a
citizen are univerſally made known, and the meaneſt
individual muſt perceive, that he is intitled to the
enjoyment of his rights and privileges, ſince he is
bound to appear in their defence.

Such ſoldiers, alſo, not being totally dedicated
to military purpoſes, except in caſes of urgent ne-
ceſſity,

cessity, can never become so uselefs a burden upon the nation, as standing forces are deservedly accounted.

Lastly, it is impossible without such an institution, to keep up for any length of time a military spirit in an industrious nation. It may, perhaps, be roused to arms on particular occasions, but the enthusiasm with which it may be inspired in dangerous emergencies, can only be of a very temporary nature; whereas we see by the experience of some years, that regulations, such as are enacted in England, will fully answer the intention of a wise Legislature. Such weak objections as are now stated against a Scotch militia, were loudly urged when the present English system was first instituted. Many able men, full of ancient prejudices, dreading even salutary innovations, and proud of appearing the *laudatores temporis acti*, objected to a plan, the utility of which is now unquestionable, tho' at first ridiculed by a Chesterfield's wit, and arraigned by the abilities of a Hardwick.

The objections which have been urged against the general principle of such a system, are by no means well founded.

By some the expence of such a military defence for Scotland is complained of, which for 6000 men would amount to 34,970 l. in time of peace, and 104,440 l. in time of war. But to this it may be answered, that it is a plan founded upon

the

the most œconomical principles of any durable
system of defence, and that no money can be
grudged which is expended for the purpose of protecting a free people from domestic tyranny, as
well as foreign depredations.

It is imagined by others, that it will be difficult
to procure the inferior officers, and even the common men. The men undoubtedly may be had,
for they are still in the country, and, indeed, it
is absurd to suppose, that in so extensive and populous a kingdom as Scotland, containing upon a
moderate calculation 300,000 fighting men, there
should be any difficulty to raise 6000 men for its
own defence*. As to the inferior officers, perhaps
some alteration ought to be made in the constitu-
tion of the Scotch militia, Perhaps even in England it might be proper to diminish the number of inferior militia officers, and to increase the
pay of such as are retained. For surely a militia,
who may possibly never see an enemy, cannot require so many officers, as may be necessary in a
standing army, one half of whom may be destroyed
in a single engagement. Nay, the inferior officers
in a militia, whose service as well as pay is merely
of a temporary nature, ought to be rather more

---

* The only alteration which occurs to me with respect
to the common men, is, that none but batchelors ought to
be ballotted for, if there are a sufficient number of that de-
scription in the district in which they are to be raised.

amply

amply paid than a body of men, who muſt receive a certain emolument from the public after their ſervices are no longer neceſſary*.

The laſt objection to ſuch an inſtitution is, that it may poſſibly prove deſtructive to induſtry. This objection appears to me peculiarly contemptible. The wealthier and the more induſtrious a nation is, the more it is expoſed to every poſſible misfortune, unleſs protected by the military ſpirit of its inhabitants. Indeed of what avail is all the wealth and induſtry imaginable, if at the ſame time means are not adopted, for the purpoſe of preſerving the fruits of that induſtry from depredation and plunder.

After conſidering this ſubject, with all the attention in my power, it appears to me, that the eſtabliſhment of a Scotch militia, on principles in general ſimilar to that of England, ought not to be any longer delayed. The ſubject is once more brought under the conſideration of parliament, and there is every reaſon to expect ſucceſs,

---

* If at any time it was found difficult to procure a ſufficient number of officers, or of men, ſuch a difficulty might be eaſily overcome, by prohibiting any perſon to ſit in either houſe of parliament, or to vote at any election, who had not ſerved for three years in ſome corps of militia, either as an officer or a ſoldier, in his own perſon, or by a ſubſtitute. As to recruiting the army, it might be done with very little difficulty, by obliging every pariſh in Scotland, and every hundred in England, for every three pariſhes it contained, to furniſh one recruit.

from

from the weaknefs of the arguments which are
urged againft it, and from the prefent temper, as
well as neceffity of the times.

The arguments which have been made ufe of
againft this neceffary meafure, by the reprefentatives of England, are. 1ft, That it would im-
pede the recruiting fervice. 2dly, That it would
endanger the liberties of England. And 3dly,
That the expence of fuch an eftablifhment, ought
to be raifed by a local tax, and ought not to be
paid out of the general revenues of the ftate.

That Scotland has long been the nurfery of the
armies of England, is a melancholy truth, which
that part of the ifland has had fufficient reafon to
regret, and to the friends of Caledonia, it is perhaps the ftrongeft objection to the eftablifhment of
a Scotch militia, that it would keep up a military
fpirit in that country, which would perpetually
fill the thinned ranks of the forces of Great-Britain. It is however certain, that if the northern
part of the ifland, is ftill to be marked by any ob-
noxious diftinction, the fpirit of the people will
be roufed, and it will not be difficult, for the
nobility and gentry of that country, to prevent
almoft any addition in future, to the number of
recruits *.

* The Scotch militia bill would have paffed ann. 1776,
had it not been for the claufe which permitted the regular
forces to recruit out of the militia of that country, which
the

That a Scotch militia of 6000 men, would endanger the liberty of England, is no great compliment to its ftability or ftrength. I hope that it is not built on fo fandy a foundation. If fo fmall a body of men however, could poffibly give any difturbance to England, it muft be much more alarmed to find that every individual profeffing the Proteftant religion, is intitled to train himfelf to arms, and that the King is empowered to demand the affiftance of 20,000 foot, and 2000 horfe, and if neceffary the fervice of every man from fixteen to fixty, to any part of his Britifh dominions, without any new act impowering him fo to do. The number above ftated, namely, 20,000 foot, and 2000 horfe, were thought neceffary for the defence of Scotland, by the parliament of that country, but at this time perhaps 6000 militia with 4000 fencibles may be fufficient. A lefs number cannot be accepted of; indeed Ireland, a country inferior in point of extent to Scotland, has always had 12,000 men for its internal protection *.

---

the reprefentatives of that part of the ifland could not poffibly affent to, unlefs the fame regulation had been extended to England.

* According to Templeman's Survey, England contains 31,648,000 acres. Scotland, 17,788,160 acres. Ireland, 17,572,480 acres: confequently Scotland is more extenfive than Ireland by 215,680 acres.

As

As to the expence of fuch an eftablifhment, which muft be paid, not by a local tax, but muft be drawn from the general revenues of the ftate, any objection of that kind, will not ftand a ferious inveftigation. Though the expence of the prefent militia in England, is paid from the land-tax; yet a land-tax was raifed in that country, long before that excellent inftitution was thought of; nor can there poffibly exift any connexion between the Englifh land-tax, and the Englifh militia, unlefs when the latter was eftablifhed, a new tax of a local nature, in addition to the ufual tax of four fhillings in the pound, had been laid upon land, for the exprefs purpofe of defraying the charges of that fpecies of protection. If the principle however is a juft one, that no one is bound to pay taxes, unlefs he is fufficiently protected, it may be faid in behalf of a Scottifh militia, *that whilft a fingle fhilling remains of the revenue which is raifed from that country, by any means whatfoever, it muft in the firft place be appropriated for its defence.* How different alfo is the behaviour of England, to other parts of the Britifh empire. When the Colonies of North America rebelled, they were told, give us your trade, and we will pay for your protection. It is well known what advantages Ireland has lately received without any apparent compenfation. But

when

when the defence of Scotland is brought upon the carpet, tho' its trade is fo beneficial to England*, tho' it is the great nurfery of its naval and military ftrength, and though it pays a revenue of above half a million per annum †, yet any expence that can be laid out upon that country, tho' raifed from Scotland itfelf, become the immediate fource of jealoufy and regret. At a time however, when there is reafon to hope that every national diftinction is on the brink of being exploded, it

---

* " What we lofe by France, fays Sir Thomas Clifford, " we gain upon Scotland. *Scotland is our Indies* ; as Colbert " calls England the King of France's Indies." Grey's Debates, vol. 1. p. 59. The fingle article of broad cloth, draws half a million per annum from Scotland to England.

† The following is fuppofed to be the annual revenue raifed from Scotland :

	£.
Cuftoms	120,000
Excife	150,000
Land-Tax	48,000
Poft-Office	20,000
Stamps, &c.	25,000
Eaft India goods, groceries, &c. paid in the ports of England for Scotland	150,000
	513,000

This is exclufive of the advantages which England receives by a moft beneficial trade with Scotland, and by having above one-half of the rents of that country expended in England. But above all, by furnifhing fo large a proportion of men, as has enabled England hitherto to carry on extenfive wars, without injuring her commerce or manufactures.

would

would be improper to dwell upon the exiftence
of unfortunate prejudices, which are daily paffing
away.

That the ablefl men of both countries, taking
into their moft ferious confideration, the fubjects
treated of in this little eflay, may contrive the
means of placing the military ftrength of the
empire, upon a firm and ftable bafis, and that
every national prejudice, and every unreafonable
diftinction may be done away, is the fincere wifh
of one, who will ever be willing to contribute his
mite to the profperity of his country.

T H E   E N D.

www.ingramcontent.com/pod-product-compliance
Lightning Source LLC
Chambersburg PA
CBHW022146090426
42742CB00010B/1412